What Is Matter?

 HOUGHTON MIFFLIN HARCOURT

Printed in Mexico

ISBN: 978-0-544-07314-2

6 7 8 9 10 0908 21 20 19 18 17 16

4500608014   A B C D E F G

Be an Active Reader!

 Look at these words.

matter	density	condensation
temperature	solid	mixture
magnetism	liquid	solution
mass	gas	
volume	evaporation	

 Look for answers to these questions.

What can we observe about matter?

What is temperature?

What is magnetism?

How can we measure matter?

Why do some objects float?

Why do some objects sink?

How can we classify water?

How does heating change water?

How does cooling change water?

How can matter change?

What is a mixture?

What is a solution?

What can we observe about matter?

Everything you see around you is made of matter. Matter is anything that has mass and takes up space. Our senses of sight, hearing, taste, smell, and touch help us observe the physical properties of matter. These properties include hardness, color, taste, size, shape, odor, and texture.

Observe an apple. It's red, round, and about the same size as the palm of your hand. The apple is hard, but it's not too hard to bite! You can taste the sugary juice and smell the sweetness of the fruit. These are physical properties that describe the apple. They are some of the many properties of matter.

An apple is made of matter.

What is temperature?

Temperature is a measure of how hot or cold something is. It is a physical property of matter that we measure with a thermometer.

There are two scales, or systems, that measure temperature. On the Celsius scale, water freezes at 0 °C and boils at 100 °C. On the Fahrenheit scale, water freezes at 32 °F and boils at 212 °F.

When something has a low temperature, it feels cold. On a snowy day in January, an air temperature of –6.6 °C (20 °F) feels very cold. When something has a high temperature, it feels hot. If the air temperature on a day in August is 43.3 °C (110 °F), you feel very hot!

Fahrenheit and Celsius are different temperature scales. Each scale marks water's freezing and boiling points differently.

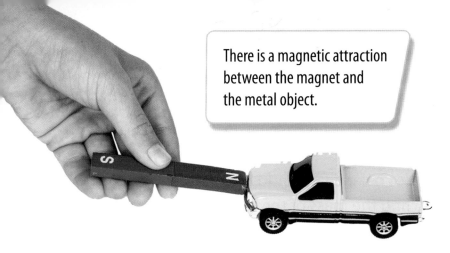

There is a magnetic attraction between the magnet and the metal object.

What is magnetism?

Magnetism is the physical property that allows a material to become a magnet or be attracted by a magnet. A magnet is an object that attracts some kinds of metals, like iron. Long ago, people discovered that a rock called lodestone was magnetic. People used lodestones to make magnets.

Iron, steel, and nickel are metals that are all attracted by magnets. If you put any one of these metals near a magnet, it will be attracted to the magnet, or pulled in by it.

Most materials are not magnetic. Wood is not magnetic. If you put a magnet near a piece of wood, the wood will not move toward the magnet. Paper, plastic, and glass are also not magnetic.

How can we measure matter?

Mass is the amount of matter an object has. You can measure an object's mass with a pan balance. First, you put the object you want to measure on one side of the pan balance. Then you put known masses on the other side until the two sides balance. You add the numbers of the known masses to find the mass of the object.

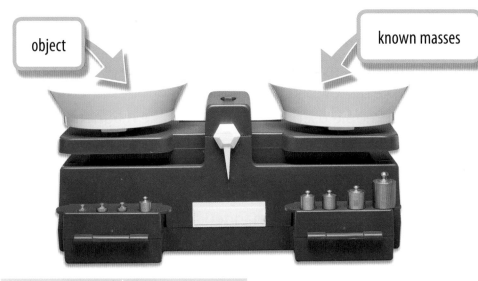

object

known masses

Object	Mass
toothbrush	28 g
tomato	170.8 g
book	226.7 g
sneaker	311.8 g

This chart shows the mass of some common objects.

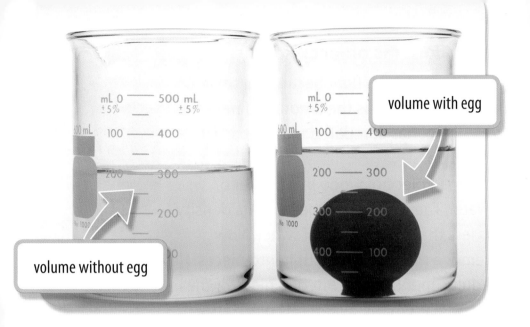

volume with egg

volume without egg

Volume is the amount of space that an object takes up. You can use a beaker of water to measure an object's volume. Let's measure the volume of an egg. Put 300 ml of water in a beaker. When you put the egg in the beaker, the water level increases to 350 ml. The volume of the egg has increased the water level. Subtract the two numbers to find the egg's volume. The volume of the egg is 50 ml.

A metric ruler is a good tool to use to measure the volume of a rectangular solid such as a book. The width of a book is 15 cm. Its length is 23 cm and its height is 5 cm. Multiply the numbers. $15 \times 23 \times 5 = 1,725$. The volume of the book is 1,725 cubic centimeters.

Why do some objects float?

Some objects float because of their density. Density is the amount of matter an object has compared to the space it takes up.

Put a piece of wood in a beaker of water. The wood floats because its density is less than the density of water. Now remove the wood and cut it into pieces. Have an adult supervise you. Put one piece of the wood back in the water. This piece also floats, because a small piece of an object has the same density as the whole object.

These objects are all less dense than water, so each will float:

- plastic bottle cap
- piece of wax
- cork
- wooden block
- piece of dental floss
- plastic bag

What other objects might float in water?

The marble is more dense than water.

Why do some objects sink?

Every object is made up of tiny particles of matter. When these particles are close together, the object has more density. Objects that are more dense than water will sink.

Put a marble in a beaker of water. The marble sinks because its density is more than the density of water. Sometimes two similar objects can have different densities. A table tennis ball and a golf ball are both balls. However, a golf ball has a greater density, so it will sink.

Each of these objects will sink because it is more dense than water.

- penny or other coin
- marble
- golf ball
- bar of soap
- paper clip
- peanut

How can we classify water?

We can classify water by its three states of matter—solid, liquid, and gas. When water is in a solid state, it has a definite volume and shape. An ice cube is solid water that is usually rectangular or square in shape. A snowball is round, solid water.

Have you gone ice-skating? The ice is a solid that takes the shape of the rink. A glacier is a large body of frozen water. It is also a solid. A tiny snowflake is also solid water.

A snowflake is water in a solid state.

When water is in a liquid state, it has a definite volume, but not a definite shape. The water takes the shape of the container that holds it. A swimming pool is full of liquid water that takes the shape of the pool. Rain is liquid water in the form of tiny drops.

Water can also be a gas called water vapor. You can't see gas. A gas does not have a definite volume or a definite shape. It will expand to fill all the space in a container. The container may be small, like a bicycle tire that has been pumped with air. Or the space may be large, like a room.

Water can change from one state to another. It can change from a liquid to a solid, from a solid to a liquid, or from a liquid to a gas.

The river is liquid water. The air contains water vapor.

Solid water in the form of ice can change states and become liquid water.

How does heating change water?

The temperature of water increases when heat energy increases. Suppose you take an ice cube out of the freezer and put it in a dish on the kitchen table. The ice cube starts to warm up. The particles in the ice cube move apart, and the ice cube melts. Melting is a physical change from a solid to a liquid state.

Large bodies of solid water can also melt. Picture a warm day in March. A frozen lake receives an increase in heat energy from the sun, warming the ice. The ice begins to melt as it changes from a solid to a liquid state. You can't ice skate on melting ice!

The process by which a liquid changes into a gas is called evaporation. As heat energy warms water, the particles of the water all move faster. Particles in the water bump into particles on top of the water. The particles on the top go into the air and turn into a gas.

When the water temperature increases, evaporation speeds up. The particles of water move around even more. They form bubbles of water vapor that move to the surface and form steam. The steam evaporates into the air.

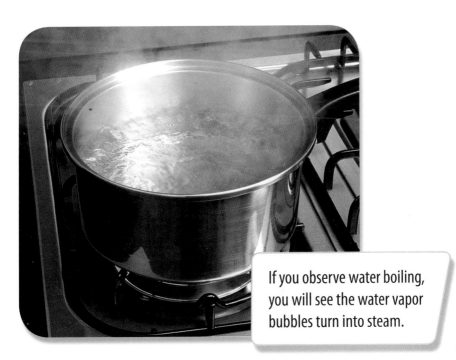

If you observe water boiling, you will see the water vapor bubbles turn into steam.

How does cooling change water?

The temperature of water decreases when there is less heat energy. Suppose you fill an empty ice cube tray with liquid water and put the tray in the freezer. The low temperature in the freezer causes a physical change to the water. The particles in the water move closer together, and the water freezes. Now you have solid water in the form of ice cubes.

Very large amounts of liquid water can also freeze. Picture a pond on a cold day in December. The pond is liquid water. When the temperature decreases due to less heat energy from the sun, the liquid water begins to turn to ice. If the temperature continues to decrease, more ice will form.

Water changes from a liquid to a solid state when it freezes.

Cooling changes water vapor to liquid water. The process by which a gas changes into a liquid is called condensation.

Suppose you put ice cubes and liquid water together in a glass. The outside of the glass is dry. Wait a few minutes, though, and you will observe tiny drops of water forming on the outside of the glass. Some of the water vapor in the air has condensed on the cold glass and changed to liquid water.

How do clouds form? Warm air containing water vapor moves upward into cooler air temperatures. As the warm air cools, the water vapor condenses. It forms drops of water that come together and form clouds.

Water vapor in the air condenses on a cold glass, changing to liquid water.

Cutting an apple causes a physical change. But the apple doesn't change into something else.

How can matter change?

Physical changes to matter do not change the substance. For example, slicing an apple causes a physical change in the apple. The size and shape change, but it's still an apple. If you fold a rectangular tissue into a square, it's still a tissue.

You've seen that matter can exist in different states: solid, liquid, and gas. Matter can change states and still remain the same substance. Melting causes a change of state. A dish of ice cream on a table begins to warm up and starts to melt. The ice cream is in a liquid state, but it's still ice cream.

Freezing causes a change of state. When you put a container of liquid soup in the freezer, the soup changes from a liquid to a solid, but it's still soup.

Matter can be reused or recycled. You can reuse an aluminum can by making it into a pencil holder. Just clean out the can and decorate the outside. You can also reuse a plastic bottle and change it into a flower pot. First, cut off the top. Then, put dirt in the bottom and add some flower seeds or a small plant.

A lot of used paper gets recycled. The old paper is shredded and mixed into a pulp. The pulp becomes new newspapers, paper plates, or toilet paper.

Glass can be recycled over and over. Melted glass is used for new jars, glasses, or windows. Crushed glass may be used in bricks or in paving for a road.

Recycled plastic has many uses. Your old bottles may become part of a swing set! Many toys are made from recycled plastic.

What ways can you think of to recycle and reuse newspaper?

How many substances can you identify in this mixture?

What is a mixture?

A mixture is a combination of two or more different substances that retain their identities. Each substance stays the same. A new substance is not formed. Forming a mixture is a physical change. Solids, liquids, and gases can all form mixtures.

When you add fruit to your cereal, you have a mixture of two solids. If you add milk, you have a mixture of two solids and one liquid.

Mixtures occur all the time and in all kinds of places. Many rocks are a mixture of minerals. Each of the minerals might be visible in the rock.

Here's how to make your own mixture. Put some sand in a pail and add some rocks. Stir or shake the pail. If you lift a handful of the mixture, the sand will fall through your fingers. The rocks will stay in your hand. The rocks and sand each retain their own identity.

Make another mixture. Put some sand in a jar and add water. Put on the lid and shake it up. At first, the water and sand look like they are mixed together. However, let the jar sit still for a few minutes. The sand will sink to the bottom. The water and sand each retain their own identity.

How can you tell that each substance in this mixture keeps its own identity?

What is a solution?

A solution is a mixture that has the same composition throughout because the particles of each substance are spread out evenly. A solvent is the larger part of a solution that dissolves other substances. Water is a common solvent. A substance that dissolves in a solvent is called a solute. For example, sugar is a solute that dissolves in water, a solvent.

A solution can be a mixture of a solid and a liquid. The result will be a liquid. When you mix solid chocolate powder with liquid milk, you get liquid chocolate milk.

A solution can be a liquid and another liquid. Rubbing alcohol is a solution. It is a mixture of water and another liquid called isopropanol.

A solution can be a gas and a liquid. Carbon dioxide is a gas. When you mix it with water, you get carbonated water, also called soda water.

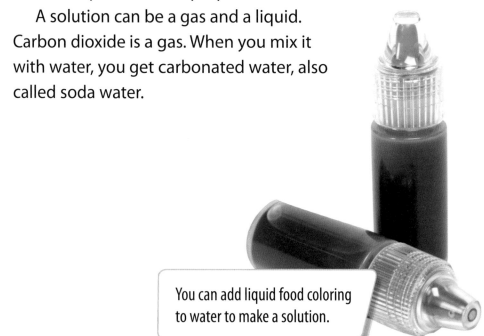

You can add liquid food coloring to water to make a solution.

Green food coloring, a solute, combines with water, a solvent, to form a solution.

A solution can be made with two melted solids that are mixed together. A penny is made from copper and zinc. A dime is made from copper and nickel.

Here's how to make a solution. Put some sugar in a jar. The sugar is the solute. Add water, which is the solvent. As you shake the jar, you see the solid and liquid begin to mix. Put the jar on the table and let it sit for a few minutes. You can't tell the water from the sugar. They have mixed evenly, so you know they are a solution.

Observe Sinking and Floating

Investigate sinking and floating. Collect some objects from home or school. They should be made of a variety of materials and should have different sizes, shapes, and textures. Fill a sink or large bowl about halfway with water. Create a three-column chart and write the name of each object in the left column of the chart. Make a prediction about whether each object will sink or float. Record your prediction in the middle column. Put each object in the water and record the results in the right column. Was your prediction correct? Write a paragraph that describes your findings.

Write a Report

Use the Internet or library resources to learn more about how water changes states. Write a report that describes how water changes from a solid to a liquid, from a liquid to a gas, and from a liquid to a solid. Include a diagram with labels that explains how each process occurs.

Glossary

condensation [kahn•duhn•SAY• shuhn] The process by which a gas changes into a liquid.

density [DEN•suh•tee] The amount of matter in an object compared to the space it takes up.

evaporation [ee•vap•uh•RAY•shuhn] The process by which a liquid changes into a gas.

gas [GAS] The state of matter that does not have a definite shape or volume.

liquid [LIK•wid] The state of matter that has a definite volume but no definite shape.

magnetism [MAG•ni•tiz•uhm] The physical property of being magnetic.

mass [MASS] The amount of matter an object has.

matter [MAT•er] Anything that has mass and takes up space.

mixture [MIKS•cher] A combination of two or more different substances that retain their identities.

solid [SAHL•id] The state of matter that has a definite shape and a definite volume.

solution [suh•LOO•shun] A mixture that has the same composition throughout because all the parts are mixed evenly.

temperature [TEM•pur•uh•chur] A measure of how hot or cold something is.

volume [VAHL•yoom] The amount of space that an object takes up.